MORE
TRULY STUPID
SPORTS
QUOTES

Also by Jeff Parietti:

*The Book of Truly Stupid
Business Quotes*

*The Book of Truly Stupid
Sports Quotes*

MORE
TRULY STUPID
SPORTS
QUOTES

JEFF PARIETTI

HarperPerennial
A Division of HarperCollins*Publishers*

HarperCollins books may be purchased for educational, business, or sales promotional use. For information, please write to: Special Markets Department, HarperCollins Publishers, Inc., 10 East 53rd Street, New York, New York 10022.

Library of Congress Cataloging-in-Publication Data

Parietti, Jeff.
     More truly stupid sports quotes / Jeff Parietti
          p.   cm.
     ISBN 0–06–273647–7
     1. Sports personnel—Quotations.   2. Sports—Quotations, maxims, etc.
3. Sports—Humor. I. Title.
GV707.P346   1999
796'.02'07—dc21   98-51521
                                                                                       CIP

---

99 00 01 02 03 ❖/RRD 10 9 8 7 6 5 4 3 2 1

CONTENTS

PREFACE

Welcome to the latest in a series of books emerging from The Quote Zone! Prepare to depart on an adventurous journey through team locker rooms, broadcast booths, post-game interview facilities and other places where humorous, witty, sarcastic and just plain truly stupid sports quotes are uttered.

I selected the best material from hundreds of quotes compiled during an intensive research process. (Local librarians saw me so often they almost gave me my own key.) To maintain each quotation's original context, team affiliations and titles are listed as of the time the individual made the comment.

So, put up the ol' feet after a hard day's work, take a break from the homework, turn off the television, and flip to any page to find some humor from The Quote Zone.

Just a few final thoughts: In life, it's always important to thank those who help you along the way. I'd like to thank my family, relatives, friends and co-workers for their support. Special thanks to all the hard-working professionals on the HarperCollins team who made this project a reality.

And a hearty "thank you" to all you readers for making my previous two works with HarperCollins—*The Book of Truly Stupid Sports Quotes* and *The Book of Truly Stupid Business Quotes*—such successes. May you find much enjoyment and laughter from this book.

Jeff Parietti
March 1999

Chapter 1

PLAY BY PLAY

"There's a soft liner, which is caught by the second baseman. And the ball game is over—for this inning."

—Jerry Coleman, San Diego Padres announcer, describing action in bottom of ninth inning during tie game between Padres and Reds

"Coming on to pitch is Mike Moore, who is 6-foot–1 and 212 years old."

—Herb Score, Cleveland Indians broadcaster

"Wrigley Field—it sort of reminds you of some of the old ballparks."

—CBS Radio broadcaster Jeff Torborg

"And the ball is out of here. No, it's not. Yes, it is. No, it's not. What happened?"

—New York Yankees broadcaster Phil Rizzuto, vainly attempting to describe events surrounding long fly ball that was caught

"One of the all-time greatest players of all-time in this game."

—Pittsburgh Pirates announcer Bob Walk on pitcher Steve Carlton

"Oxford are ahead. No, Cambridge are ahead. I don't know who's ahead, but it's either Oxford or Cambridge."

—BBC announcer John Snagge, famed for this enlightening play-by-play of 1949 Oxford–Cambridge crew race

"David Cone is the only Mets pitcher who has a pinch hit as a pinch-hitter."

—Ralph Kiner, New York Mets broadcaster

"He's one of the hardest workers on this team. He's had his ear to the grindstone all season."

—St. Louis Cardinals broadcaster Mike Shannon,
sizing up a player

"He'll take your head off at the blink of a hat."

—Color analyst Joe Theismann, on an NFL draft pick

"Our hats go off to drug abusers everywhere."

—Jerry Coleman, San Diego Padres broadcaster, commenting on the fight against drug abuse

"And he hits one in the hole. They're going to have to hurry. They'll never get him! They got him. How do you like that? Holy cow! I changed my mind before he got there so that doesn't count as an error."

—Phil Rizzuto, New York Yankees broadcaster

"Half of Jeff King's extra-base hits last year were extra-base hits."

—Ralph Kiner

"Oh my God, I have to go to the bathroom."

—College hoop analyst George Raveling, during exciting final minute of Arizona's close win over UCLA

"Next up is Fernando Gonzalez, who isn't playing tonight."

—Jerry Coleman

"He's on about the 40, the 50, 51, 52-yard line."

—Dave Rowe of Raycom Network, on pass reception
and run by TCU's Curtis Modkins

"The most inexpensive—uh, inexperienced—part of the defense."

—NBC sportscaster Charlie Jones, describing Nebraska's
secondary in 1990 Fiesta Bowl

"The biggest sports crowd in the state of Atlanta."

—Canadian Mark Jones, ABC announcer, on attendance at University of Georgia's 1991 inaugural contest in expanded Sanford Stadium

"This time he grounds it on the ground."

—Ralph Kiner, on a little dribbler to shortstop by Gary Redus

"Wasn't watching."

—Noted talker Phil Rizzuto, on why the heck he had written a "ww" in his score book following an at-bat

Chapter 2

YOU DON'T SAY!

"That might have been the best game you ever pitched."

—Yogi Berra to Don Larsen, following his 1956 World Series perfect game

"The way I play, I'd set the game back 100 yards."

—Bill Peterson, Florida State football coach, turning down invitation to play golf

"We'll be working nine to five. We'll be like those people in Pittsburgh working in those steel mines."

—New York forward Xavier McDaniel, on how Knicks planned to tackle Chicago Bulls in playoffs

"Lance Johnson [of the Mets] has a chance to do something that's never been done. He can lead the American League in hits. And he has already done that."

—New York Mets broadcaster Ralph Kiner, during the National League team's final series of season

"I'm not blind to hearing what everybody else hears."

—Boston lefty Zane Smith, regarding rumors he wouldn't be on Red Sox playoff roster

"I've won at every level, except college and pro."

—Shaquille O'Neal

"We're still shooting ourselves in the mouth."

> —Alabama wide receiver Marcel West,
> discussing Crimson Tide mistakes

"I misquoted myself."

> —Forward Andrew DeClercq, retreating from statement that
> he'd leave Golden State Warriors if changes weren't made

**"I don't care what the tape says.
I didn't say it."**

> —Ray Malavasi, Los Angeles Rams coach

"Most of the time, I don't even know what I said until I read about it. But I really didn't say everything I said."

—Yogi Berra

"I don't need the ball to score."

—Charlotte Hornets forward Anthony Mason

"Introducing the only man to hold three titles simultaneously and at the same time. . . ."

—Harry Balogh, Madison Square Garden's boxing
P.A. announcer in 1930s, introducing triple champion
Henry Armstrong

"When you don't let in any goals, you have a pretty good chance to win."

—Tampa Bay goalie Corey Schwab, following 3–0 shutout of Los Angeles Kings

"It's the safest thing in the world, but it could kill you."

—Pro high diver John Maxson, on dangers of diving into pool from 80 feet high

"It's a no-win, no-lose situation."

—Pittsburgh Steelers coach Bill Cowher, possibly referring to a tie

"We're big guys and the chairs aren't real strong. Some were broken while we were just sitting on them, playing cards."

—U.S. hockey team player Doug Wright, explaining damage to some teammates' hotel rooms after elimination from 1998 Winter Olympics

"Naw, as long as you don't get lost."

—Goalie Thomas Ravelli, asked whether it was difficult to find way around town after moving from Sweden to join Tampa Bay Mutiny of Major League Soccer

"I'm not saying I'm the mastermind behind this, but I'm the mastermind behind this."

—Undefeated heavyweight boxer Crawford Grimsley, on surprise signing to face George Foreman

"Jerry Rice is the greatest, and I'm the best."

—Wide receiver Andre Rison

"It was the best he's ever made me look bad."

—Atlanta outfielder Lonnie Smith, following an 0-for-4 day against San Diego pitcher Bruce Hurst

"The Marines are the best fighting guys in the United States Army."

—Don King, on boxer Riddick Bowe joining Marine Corps Reserve

> **"I think this is the ultimate, except for the day I was born."**
>
> —Todd White, Virginia defensive tackle, following Cavaliers' upset victory over Florida State

> **"My marriage, the birth of my children, my first day in the big leagues. . . all pale in comparison to this."**
>
> —Philadelphia Phillies pitcher Dave Leiper, on first batting-practice homer of career

> **"What does it hurt to ask? All they can say is yes or no, and I already know the answer."**
>
> —Bill Pulsipher, lefty hurler for Mets' Norfolk (Va.) Triple A team, on planning to ask for a call-up or trade

**"I've got a thing called Majors' law:
It doesn't catch up with you until it
catches up with you."**

—Johnny Majors, Pittsburgh Panthers grid coach

Chapter 3

DUMB ADMISSIONS

"It was a great feeling to run around like an idiot."

—Fred Couples on celebrating his putt that clinched Presidents Cup for U.S. squad

"We've got to keep Mel dumb."

—Detroit Tigers skipper Buddy Bell, ordering outfielder Melvin Nieves to quit viewing videotapes of at-bats, because the more he analyzes, the more he whiffs

"I'm convinced he's smart enough to play with any dumb jock out there."

—District court judge Daniel Schneider, ruling for New Mexico hoop recruit Kenny Thomas, who sued NCAA for declaring him academically ineligible

"It's how they want us. . . big, strong and dumb."

—Jim McKenzie, Phoenix Coyotes enforcer, on why he played
five games with broken bone in his leg

"I think offensive linemen, in general, would be offended if you called them sophisticated."

—Dave Shula, Cincinnati Bengals coach, queried about
his offensive line's sophistication

"One guy had a real low test score, so we decided to go back and check the interviews. In one of them, he said he was raised by wolves."

—Jimmy Johnson, Miami Dolphins coach, on an unusual NFL draft experience

"I don't think anyone is smart enough to fall for that."

—Buffalo right wing Matthew Barnaby, after Washington Capitals coach Ron Wilson tried to goad Sabres by calling them "chicken"

"This year, we have a physical masseuse. Last year, we needed a mental masseuse."

—New Jersey forward Jayson Williams,
on team's marked improvement

"You can be stupid once, but idiotic to do it again. I'll settle for being stupid."

—St. Louis Cardinals manager Tony La Russa, refusing to predict
a division title after earlier such guarantee flopped

"I don't know if we've had any mentality this year."

—Detroit quarterback Scott Mitchell, asked about Lions' mental attitude for upcoming game against Kansas City

"They're getting dumber. They run like deer, they jump like deer, and they think like deer."

—Charles Barkley, analyzing newest group of NBA players

Chapter 4

THE NUMBERS GAME

"We've had some help from the Phillies. What have they lost, nine of their last eight?"

—Ted Turner, using creative math to explain how his Atlanta Braves team had caught Philadelphia in standings

"The average attendance at Cubs games this year is 48 degrees."

—Harry Caray, Chicago Cubs broadcaster

"I usually take a two-hour nap from 1 to 4."

—Yogi Berra

"He's the only guy I know who can drive in three runs with nobody on base."

—Texas Ranger second sacker Mark McLemore, regarding RBI machine Juan Gonzalez knocking in 101 runs by 1998 All-Star break

"Two out of three ain't bad."

—Then-Dallas Cowboys president Tex Schramm, hearing that Duane Thomas, team's running back, had called him "a liar, a thief and a crook"

"I wanted to get that zero off my back. It was weighing me down."

—Forward Shawn Kemp, on switching his number from 40 to 4 upon joining Cleveland Cavaliers from Seattle Sonics

"I thought I'd be shot or hung by the time I was 40 anyway, so it's no big deal."

—Veteran NFL coach Bill Parcells,
on occasion of his 53rd birthday

"The good thing is, I don't have to play Tiger Woods until I'm 90."

—Pro golfer Chi Chi Rodriguez

"It was real big. On a scale of 1 to 10, it was a 55."

—Oregon guard Kenya Wilkins, enumerating on Ducks' upset win against 13th-ranked Fresno State

"He's just 6-foot-12, that's all."

—Minnesota Timberwolves coach Flip Saunders,
on Kevin Garnett's reluctance to admit growing to 7 feet
for fear of being labeled inside player

"Four—I can't eat eight."

—Yogi Berra, on whether he wanted his pizza cut into
eight or four pieces

"It was a hole-in-one contest, and
I had a three."

—Veteran college hoop coach Abe Lemons, on being
two shots from winning a new car

"It's called an eraser."

—Arnold Palmer, on how to take five strokes off your golf game

"Sure, I've got one. It's a perfect 20–20."

—Duane Thomas, then-Dallas Cowboy and Super Bowl star running back, asked about his IQ

"It changed 360 percent."

—Bora Milutinovic, U.S. soccer coach, trying to explain growing interest in 1994 World Cup played in America

"My earned-run average is so high, it looks like an AM radio station."

—Journeyman pitcher Jim Gott

"I've only got two words: It ain't no surprise."

—Denver cornerback Darrien Gordon, after Broncos won Super Bowl over Green Bay

Chapter 5

VOCABULARY & SPELLING

"Omar Vizquel sympathizes everything that's good about the Cleveland Indians."

—Jim Thome, accepting award for teammate Vizquel

"He had the most incredible misdemeanor."

—PGA Tour player Fulton Allen, on 19-year-old amateur Matt Kuchar's composure at 1998 Masters

"My kids and my wife are here, so we'll go on some tours of the Luge, probably some shopping."

—Michael Jordan, actually referring to the Louvre, while in Paris with Chicago Bulls for game

"They asked me to spell Mississippi. I said, 'Which one? The state or the river?'"

—Providence basketball coach Pete Gillen, on taking spelling test to get into college

"Down the left-field and right-field lines, it's 99 liters, whatever that means."

—Broadcaster Ralph Kiner, during Mets game at Montreal's Olympic Stadium

"It was way, way out. If this were the '60s, I'd say it was far out."

—Florida Marlins scout Gary Hughes, on 450-foot homer by Class AA catcher Charles Johnson in 1994

"I've been rebounding all year like this, so what's the big thing? If it took him this long to figure it out, I'd hate to sit here and do a crossword puzzle with him."

—New Jersey Net Jayson Williams, hearing that coach Butch Beard was thinking about making him a starter because of his rebounding skills

"He was disqualified for bad spelling."

—Tom Sweeney, New York City Marathon competitor, after runner's counterfeit number read "maraton" instead of "marathon"

"Don't ask me. I need a dictionary with English, Finnish and Tikkanese."

—New York Rangers goalie Mike Richter, on what Finnish teammate Esa Tikkanen said after game-winning playoff goal

"That's the difference between this year and last year. This year, he has a funny interpreter."

—New York Yankees shortstop Derek Jeter, on seeing pitcher Hideki Irabu laugh at teammate's joke after it was translated

"A lot of people think it's going to take the mustard off the World Series. Well, the World Series will always have mustard on it. Anytime you're playing for that ring, there's going to be mustard involved."

—Veteran reliever Lee Smith, on whether interleague-play introduction would take "luster" off World Series

"Gee, you've known me all those years and you still don't know how to spell my name."

—Yogi Berra, upon receiving check that said "Payable to Bearer"

"The young players that come out of college today, most guys can't even spell their own names. . . . Excuse me, hello, we have a vocabulary here."

—Dennis Rodman

"After a day like this, I've got the three Cs: I'm comfortable, I'm confident, and I'm seeing the ball well."

—Seattle Mariners outfielder Jay Buhner, after perfect 5-for-5 day against Yankees

"It's a big word and I don't know any big words."

—Garrett Stephenson, Philadelphia Phillies rookie pitcher, asked to explain his ailing knee

"I just hope we can do some vendetting."

—Atlanta Falcons coach Dan Reeves, on schedule's grudge games, including one versus Denver, his ex-team

"I didn't think they still had rotator phones."

—Cincinnati Reds catcher Joe Oliver, after having to dial a call while visiting teammate at Montreal's Queen Elizabeth Hospital

"We needed to buy a vowel."

—New York Mets G.M. Steve Phillips, on why organization
signed Dutch-born infielder Robert Eenhoorn

**"It was a cross between a screwball and a
change-up—a screw-up."**

—Chicago Cubs reliever Bob Patterson, on pitch he threw to
Cincinnati shortstop Barry Larkin for game-winning homer

"Really, I never tuteled that boy."

—Bum Phillips, asked about tutelage he'd given son, Wade, who
had been named Denver's head coach

"Marv's more likely to quote Homer, and I'm more likely to quote Homer Simpson."

—Buffalo Bills coach Wade Phillips, on predecessor Marv Levy

"It was regression, depression. . . It's all kinds of 'essions, a succession of 'essions, actually."

—New York Jets quarterback Boomer Esiason, on blowout loss to Oakland

"I don't speak German, he doesn't speak English, and I think I just agreed to marry his daughter."

—Safety Jeff Hammerschmidt of World League's Frankfurt Galaxy, after talking with mayor of Fischbach, Germany

Chapter 6

WHAT'S IN A NAME?

"I just looked at him right now and said, 'Do you know who I am?' He said, 'Yeah, you're Batman.'"

—Green Bay Packer coach Mike Holmgren, on checking out Robert Brooks, who suffered concussion during game

"You the Mom!"

—Anonymous fan at LPGA Oldsmobile Classic to Laura Baugh, pregnant with seventh child

"Swish Kaba!"

—Seton Hall announcer Warner Fuselle's call whenever forward Jacky Kaba makes a swish shot

"He has so many fishhooks in his nose, he looks like a piece of bait."

—NBC announcer Bob Costas, explaining why Dennis Rodman was nicknamed "The Worm"

"I told him when we started: 'When I get through with you, they'll call you No Bread Red.'"

—Minnesota Fats, on 1961 match with fellow pool hustler Cornbread Red Birge

"I'm changing my name to Da Kid. First name Da. Last name Kid."

—Kevin Garnett, Minnesota Timberwolves forward

"John Smiley is going to change his name to John Frowny."

—Cincinnati Reds coach Tony Perez, on reports that pitcher John Smiley was unhappy about trade to Minnesota from Pittsburgh

"It was a Cecil B. Demise production."

—Atlanta forward Grant Long, after Hawks lost game by blowing big lead

"Isn't he that guy with Felix Unger?"

—Charles Barkley, on Brazilian hoop star Oscar Schmidt

"At some point, they ought to call you Senior Junior."

—Mets broadcaster Ralph Kiner, to Montreal Expo Junior Nobos

"Are you James or Tiger? I can't keep it straight."

—Golfer Tom Lehman, upon running into actor James Woods at Pebble Beach pro-am tournament

"Now, they have Superman, Batman and Rodman."

—Philadelphia 76ers center Sharone Wright, on Bulls' trio of Michael Jordan, Scottie Pippen and new teammate Dennis Rodman, after Rodman got first triple-double

"They call it a golf course because all of the other four-letter words were taken."

—Raymond Floyd, ridiculing 1992 British Open course
after falling out of title chase

"This guy has been in the grass so often the chipmunks know him by name."

—ESPN sportscaster Paul Page, after Indy car driver Paul Tracy
went off course once in practice and twice in race

"You mean the great home-run hitter."

—New Jersey Net Yinka Dare, on whether he was reading
about Beirut in newspaper

"I'm sure he is in his grave right now giving a thumbs up."

—Jeff Jerome, *Poe House and Museum* curator, on Baltimore resident Edgar Allan Poe's probable reaction to NFL team's nickname choice of "Ravens"

"Kelvin Cato? Is that the guy from the O.J. trial?"

—Rick Adelman, *Golden State Warriors coach*, trying to place name of Iowa State's 6-foot-11 shot blocker

"I guess we should have picked an animal that has been extinct for 65 million years, like the Raptors."

—Vancouver Grizzlies spokesman Tom Mayenknecht, on team's nickname choice becoming embroiled in environmental crusade over endangered Grizzly bear

"If I wouldn't have passed, I'd have to change its name to Prep School."

—Ohio State grid recruit Ryan Pickett, who named his puppy Buckeye before achieving necessary SAT score in last-chance try

Chapter 7

HISTORY LESSONS

"In 1962, I was voted Minor League Player of the Year. Unfortunately, that was my second year in the majors."

—Bob Uecker, baseball broadcaster and former player

"The first fight we had was Cain and Abel. If I remember right, I had Cain."

—Boxing manager Lou Duva, recalling match with manager Al Certo in their more-than-40-year friendly rivalry

"You're going against the Yankees, some of whose grandfathers tried to kill your grandfathers in the Civil War."

—Vanderbilt football coach Dan McGugin, to players night before battle against Michigan

"This ain't like the old days, when you hear on the public address, 'Will the lady who lost her five kids come and get them? They're beating the Nets.'"

—New Jersey Net Jayson Williams, regarding team's progress

"He is so old, they didn't have history class when he went to school."

—Chicago White Sox utility man Steve Lyons, on 43-year-old teammate Carlton Fisk

"I couldn't care less about all those fiction stories about what happened in the year 1500 or 1600. Half of them aren't even true."

—Golfer John Daly, on college days and his indifference to medieval history and world literature

"Buck hit a home run so far off Bob Feller that it cleared the fence, the bleachers, a row of houses, and hit a big old water tower out there. It rained in that town for five weeks."

—Ted "Double Duty" Radcliffe, spinning tales about Buck Leonard, fellow Negro League star

"He's been out of the league so long they must have lost his scouting report. When he was playing, they probably pounded out the scouting reports on stone tablets."

—Detroit Pistons forward Grant Long, on John Long, his
40-year-old cousin, making a return to NBA with
Toronto Raptors

"His problem was that he couldn't win on the road."

—Buffalo Bills coach Marv Levy, explaining why Adolf Hitler
was stopped in Russia

"It doesn't even seem like it's this decade."

—Golfer Doug Tewell, trying to recall in 1998 how long it
seemed since his last PGA Tour event victory in 1980

"This is the greatest day for Cleveland sports fans since the invention of the polyester bowling shirt."

—Jay Leno, after Indians knocked Yankees out of playoffs in 1997

"Hitting my brother with a baseball bat."

—University of Arizona guard Jason Lee, on first sports memory

"I started out my athletic career as the ball. My brothers used to toss me around the room."

—Phoenix Suns coach Danny Ainge, on his introduction to sports

"I don't remember forgetting anything."

—Los Angeles King Tony Granato, asked about his memory after having brain surgery three months earlier

"The egg toss in Cub Scouts."

—Notre Dame linebacker Jeremy Nau, picking his most memorable sports event

"I've been fired more times than Custer's pistol."

—Veteran coach Tom McVie, on moving 60 times in 39 years due to his hockey career

"The three greatest mysteries of the 20th century are: Who stole the Lindbergh baby, who killed JFK, and who would win a foot race between Serge Zwikker and Gheorghe Muresan?"

—Charles Barkley

"Does that mean the 19th century?"

—Anonymous reporter, during media event promoting
Fight of the Century between ancient boxers George Foreman
and Larry Holmes

"Today a peacock, tomorrow
a feather duster."

—New Jersey Net Jayson Williams, on fame's fleeting nature

Chapter 8

TEAM CHEMISTRY

"Chemistry is a class you take in high school or college, where you figure out two plus two is 10, or something."

—Dennis Rodman, upon joining Chicago Bulls,
on his view of team chemistry

"I got traded for a girl. It can't get any worse than that."

—Utility infielder Keith English, exchanged for
Duluth Superior's Ila Borders, first woman to pitch in
regular-season, minor-league contest

"To Ethiopia, for a box of Froot Loops and a camel to be named later."

—Oakland A's outfielder Jose Canseco, pulled from on-deck circle to be traded, asked about his destination and deal's details by reporter

"I embarrassed myself, my team and my dog."

—Steve Parris, Pittsburgh Pirates pitcher, after getting knocked out of game in first inning

"It's almost like the werewolf syndrome. It's a full moon at home, and guys play like werewolves. Then we go on the road, and it's a lunar eclipse."

—Boston Celtics forward Ed Pinckney, on team's inconsistency

"I don't know how y'all cover, but y'all are some ugly fellas."

—Dallas receiver Michael Irvin, assessing new members of Cowboys defensive secondary on first day of practice

"If you don't get the job done, you'll see people disappear around here like Houdini or David Copperfield."

—Randall Hill, Miami Dolphins wide receiver, on coach Jimmy Johnson

"I've got [Scott] Fletcher's cleats, [Alan] Trammell's batting glove, [Danny] Bautista's bat, [Phil] Nevin's T-shirt and [Joe] Boever's glove. I guess you could say I'm a team player."

—Newly acquired infielder Steve Rodriguez, who arrived in Detroit without his equipment

"This team is so young, on our flights the stewardesses keep running out of plastic wings."

—Florida Marlins coach Rich Donnelly, on 1998 makeup of stripped down 1997 World Series champs

"There are a lot of guys available. . . . some of them are in rest homes."

—New York Jets coach Bill Parcells, on seeking veteran replacements for his injured defensive linemen

"This team is very laid back. In fact, we're so laid back, I doubt that any of us could lean forward."

—Dean Robertson, member of Great Britain's Walker Cup team

"Chico's Bail Bonds and Sterling Mortgage."

—Free agent pitcher Roger McDowell, after inking $500,000 pact with Texas Rangers, on other teams that pursued him

"Maybe a shopping spree at Victoria's Secret."

—Brian Williams, proposing way to motivate Chicago Bulls
teammate Dennis Rodman

"It would increase our attendance with just the Secret Service alone."

—Don Shaw, Stanford women's volleyball coach, on frosh
Chelsea Clinton's impact on attendance if she were to join squad

Chapter 9

COACHING
STRATEGY

"You hardly have enough time to adjust your zipper."

—Dick Vermeil, St. Louis Rams coach, on difficulty of making adjustments during 12-minute halftime

"I have no idea. Roll it up there and hope it doesn't bounce."

—Jim Leyland, Florida Marlins manager, trying to come up with strategy against Mark McGwire

"We're going to put weights in our pants."

—Purdue coach Jim Colletto, on how he planned to combat Wisconsin's offensive line, which averaged 300 pounds a player

"If you only score two runs, you've got to keep the other club at one or no runs."

—Chicago Cubs manager Jim Riggleman

"If we don't know what we're doing, [opponents] can't know what we're doing."

—Jim Wacker, University of Minnesota football coach, explaining why he decided to switch to new defensive set for upcoming season

"Everybody before me had talked about Coach Wooden's 'pyramid of success' and how they start their day with that. I start my day with an Egg McMuffin."

—Rick Majerus, Utah basketball coach, on feeling out of place addressing John Wooden Award banquet

"That's great. We'll take 29 players and let the muggers make our final cuts."

—New York skipper Bobby Valentine, upon hearing that Mets were scheduled for two exhibition games in New Orleans

"We go over positioning for relays and bunt plays. Then we play Hangman."

—New York Mets bullpen coach Dave LaRoche, explaining real reason for having bullpen blackboard

"The kind of confidence that the 82-year-old man had when he married a 25-year-old woman and bought a five-bedroom house next to an elementary school."

—Vanderbilt grid coach Woody Widenhofer, asked what he wanted team to show against Alabama

"I'm in favor of sex before, after and even during the game."

—Coach Mario Zagallo of Brazil's 1998 World Cup soccer team,
on his thoughts about banning player spouses and girlfriends
from team quarters during tourney

"Most of the time you send them a bottle of Dom Perignon when they win their first game. But our kids are so young, you send them a can of Ovaltine."

—Jim Leyland, Florida Marlins skipper, after rookie Ryan
Dempster recorded first career victory

"They recruit McDonald's All-Americans. We recruit guys who eat at McDonald's."

—Phil Martelli, St. Joseph's hoop coach, asked to compare his program with that of top-ranked Arizona

"We definitely will be improved this year. Last year we lost 10 games. This year we only scheduled nine."

—Montana State football coach Ray Jenkins, assessing squad's chances for upcoming campaign

"Very scientific. We got the number combinations from fortune cookies."

—Wayne Cashman of Tampa Bay Lightning, on method used by coaching staff to shake up three of four lines after home loss

**"No, I wouldn't want to coach five of me.
I wouldn't even want to coach one of me."**

—Rod Strickland, Washington Wizards point guard,
asked if he ever wanted to coach

**"The key to this whole business is sincerity.
Once you can fake that, you've got it made."**

—Ex-Detroit Lions coach Monte Clark, explaining way to
relate to players

"He's left-handed and he's breathing."

—Minnesota Twins skipper Tom Kelly, assessing positives
of pitcher Keith Garagozzo drafted from New York Yankees
organization

"We needed a win badly—more than food, more than sleep, more than anything."

—Gregg Popovich, San Antonio Spurs hoop coach, finally picking up victory after atrocious start to season

"Football coaches have a way to get it done, [because] if you don't get it done, you don't have to worry about getting it done, because you're done."

—Syracuse football coach Paul Pasqualoni, on job security

Chapter 10

THE COMPETITION

"At first, I said, 'Let's play for taxes.'"

—Michael Jordan, on playing golf with President Clinton

"From the time the sun rose every morning. We had seven kids and one bathroom. Now that's competition!"

—Calgary Flames coach Brian Sutter, asked if Sutter brothers had always been competitive

"Some of these guys wouldn't pour water on you if you were on fire."

—J.C. Snead, summing up his fellow pro golfers

"I'm sure it's not pleasant for players who have been on the tour for five or six years when a little brat wins against them."

—Tennis star Martina Hingis,
upon turning professional at age 14

"Look at that. They've got the name of Evander's next opponent up already."

—Trainer Lou Duva, seeing name of 96-year-old George Burns on Caesars Palace marquee, upon arriving for Holyfield's title bout against 40-something Larry Holmes

"We spend a lot of money on meal money. There's no team in this tournament that eats better than us. We've beaten them all every year."

—Utah Utes coach Rick Majerus, during 1997 NCAA tourney

"Instead of high jumping, we can have turnstile jumping. We'd win that in a second."

—Comedian Jackie Mason, on competition New Yorkers would win hands down if New York City hosted Olympics

"You can't let a passing team run the ball. When they do, you're in for a long day."

—Rice football coach Ken Hatfield, following 49–0 loss to BYU

"One word—intersections."

—Comedian Dennis Miller's proposal for spicing up
Olympic bobsled racing

**"I'm a washed-up boxer who hasn't fought
for 15 years. Do you know what that makes
me today? It makes me a contender."**

—Actor Tony Danza

Chapter 11

FRIENDLY INSULTS

"If he was on fire, he couldn't act as if he were burning."

—Shaquille O'Neal, assessing Dennis Rodman's acting ability

"We're friends. We'd probably send postcards to each other, but he can't write."

—Chicago Blackhawk Chris Chelios, on former Montreal teammate Claude Lemieux

"Don't get too carried away. All it means is that you're ugly."

—Mike Greenwell, setting Boston Red Sox teammate John Valentin straight after he was mistaken for Greenwell

"Nobody should be ranked number one who looks like he just swung from a tree."

—Tennis player Andre Agassi, on Pete Sampras

"David bought another yacht. The other one got wet."

—Pat Williams, Orlando Magic president, on NBA commissioner David Stern's newfound spending options resulting from his new five-year, $27 million pact

"He's a human rain delay."

—Oakland A's manager Art Howe, summing up slow work of Anaheim Angels rookie hurler Ryan Hancock

"Morrison proved that he is an ambidextrous fighter. He can get knocked out with either hand."

—Veteran boxing expert Bert Sugar, after heavyweight
Tommy Morrison got tagged with second defeat

"You've got a better chance of completing a pass to the Venus de Milo."

—Denver wideout Vance Johnson, a Minnesota preseason cut,
on being beaten out by Viking receiver Qadry Ismail

"He's Edward Scissorhands. He couldn't catch a cold in Alaska buck naked."

—Dallas Cowboy Emmitt Smith, on teammate defensive back Larry Brown, a few seasons before Brown's outstanding interception performance in Super Bowl

"Which would you rather have, a million dollars or Joe Oliver's head full of nickels?"

—Brett Boone, Cincinnati second sacker, suggesting that Reds catcher Oliver had large head

"As you know, Lou is a great talker. If he were God, Moses would have to send out for more tablets."

—Barry Alvarez, Wisconsin football coach, on ex-Notre Dame coach Lou Holtz

"As a teenager, Gonzo was so skinny he had to take steroids just to be on the chess team."

—Ex-teammate Greg Swindell, roasting new Detroit Tiger outfielder Luis Gonzalez at winter banquet

"Did you watch the Macy's Thanksgiving Day parade? The Fat Albert balloon sprung a leak, and at the last minute was replaced by Yankee first baseman Cecil Fielder."

—David Letterman

"That is one incredible year for the Bulls— or 10 incredible years for the Clippers."

—Jay Leno, following Chicago's NBA single-season record 70th victory

"At North Carolina, we have culture. At State, they have agriculture."

—Houston Rockets guard Kenny Smith, razzing teammate Chucky Brown about their respective universities, University of North Carolina and North Carolina State

"Sparky's the only guy I know who's written more books than he has read."

—Hall of Fame broadcaster Ernie Harwell, on release of retired manager Sparky Anderson's third book

"He put together a very difficult jigsaw puzzle in 18 months. Now, we've got to be impressed, because on the box it says 3 to 5 years."

—Lou Holtz, roasting former Notre Dame wide receiver Derrick Mayes at banquet

"No, Reggie, that's just your ego."

—Ex-hoop Star Cheryl Miller, to her Indiana Pacers brother, disputing his claims that his newly won Olympic gold medal was bigger than hers

"He's got two moves, folks. Forward and backward."

—Former New York Knick Walt Frazier, on 7-foot-7 Washington center Gheorghe Muresan

"He couldn't hit a curveball with an ironing board."

—Bob Feller, giving his straight scoop on Michael Jordan's attempt at baseball career

"He's the most organized individual in the world. He probably vacuums in straight lines."

—Golfer Brad Faxon, on British Open champion Justin Leonard

"Some defensive-minded, some offensive-minded and some no-minded."

—Arizona Cardinals quarterback Boomer Esiason, analyzing his six coaches in six seasons

"How can you foul out when you don't guard anyone?"

—Syracuse hoop coach Jim Boeheim, on Orangemen's Lawrence Moten

"He is like one of those guys who, when a bus crashes, he gets on to get the insurance money."

—New Jersey Net forward Jayson Williams, pondering legitimacy of a teammate's extended injury absence

"We knew the Army Cadets were involved because they cut through two fences to get to the goats, and 15 feet away there was an unlocked gate."

—Tom Bates, Navy sports information director, on team suddenly missing three mascot goats before Army-Navy grid battle

"If they can keep his wheelchair greased and his walker handy, he'll do fine."

—Dallas Mavericks coach Dick Motta, upon 60-year-old Bill Fitch becoming head coach of Los Angeles Clippers

"You start your soft-boiled eggs by the time he's ready."

—Pro golfer Johnny Miller, on Nick Faldo's very slow and deliberate approach to putting

"The speed gun on [him] is like an hourglass."

—Broadcaster Vin Scully, on Los Angeles Dodgers knuckleball pitcher Tom Candiotti

Chapter 12

OFFICIAL BUSINESS

"No. Kick them, but not necessarily spit on them."

—John Elway, asked whether he ever had urge to spit on an official

"Umpiring is best described as the profession of standing between two 7-year-olds with one ice cream cone."

—Ron Luciano, former major league umpire

"I was a victim of circumcision."

—Pittsburgh Pirates pitching coach Pete Vukovich, after his ejection for getting into beef with first base umpire Randy Marsh

"It will be the first time in boxing annals that the referee's instructions will be 'Shake hands and come out breathing.'"

—Comedian Earl Hochman, on
George Foreman–Larry Holmes bout

"If I had bad breath, he would call a foul on that."

—Dennis Rodman, on his difficulty with referee Terry Durham

"I like to watch good track competitions, particularly the young athletes, but I've had it up to here with the pee pee."

—IAAF president Primo Nebiolo, on efforts put into drug testing by the international track and field body

"I'm leading the league in technicals. Better to be silent and be a fool rather than to open your mouth and remove all doubt."

—Charles Barkley

"Come to games and boo the referees."

—Veteran NBA official Earl Strom, who was hanging up the whistle, on how he planned to spend his retirement

"First of all, I think dementia is important."

—Dee Kantner, on requirements for becoming one of first women to officiate in NBA

"I guess we shouldn't be patting them on the bottom anymore."

—Michael Jordan, on etiquette changes due with addition of NBA's first female refs

Chapter 13

THE PRESS

"I said, 'So, Michael, can one man defeat the Lakers in this series?' To which Jordan replied, 'No, because we're playing the Celtics tonight, Pat.'"

—Sportscaster Pat O'Brien, on embarrassing moment
in his first TV interview with Michael Jordan

"Is LSD back?"

—Bill Parcells, after reporter asked whether he thought
Meadowlands should be changed to Parcells-land if he led
New York Jets to Super Bowl

"It's expected he'll be given two choices for his punishment—either a year in jail or six months announcing Clipper games."

—Jay Leno, on broadcaster Marv Albert

"As long as I've got my cup on."

—Red Sox manager Jimy Williams, asked if he'd field questions by Boston's hard-hitting press corps before spring training facility opened every morning

"One guy asked me if my arms had always been this long. I told him that, no, they had grown, just like the rest of me."

—Former Boston Celtic Kevin McHale, recalling a crazy media question at NBA Finals interview session

"It's a muscle pull, pull in the oblique. That's a muscle on your side. Or, for you reporters, about where your third spare tire would be."

—New Jersey Net Jayson Williams, explaining his stomach injury

"The best three years of a sportswriter's life are the third grade."

—George Raveling, college hoop analyst and ex-coach

"I just wanted to see what happens when one mule confronts 300 asses."

—Oakland A's owner Charles O. Finley on bringing team mule, Charlie O., to World Series lunch for baseball writers

"Here's $20. Bury two."

—Alabama grid coach Bear Bryant, asked to donate $10 to help bury deceased and penniless sportswriter

"Then how about halftime?"

—Reporter for Japan's Fuji TV, after informed post-game interview with Mark McGwire might be impossible

"Good evening, and welcome to the end of our careers."

—Host Keith Olbermann's opening words upon debut of ESPN2

"The way things are going up there, before too long, they'll be blaming me for the ball going through [Bill] Buckner's legs."

—New York Jets coach Bill Parcells, on treatment by Boston press since he left New England Patriots

"I try to have respect for people in general, whether it's baseball players or lowlifes in the media."

—Jim Riggleman, upon becoming new manager of Chicago Cubs

Chapter 14

OWNERS' CORNER

"They can bring it in their tummies."

—Ted Turner, on rule at Turner Field in Atlanta that prohibited fans from carrying in their own food

"I'll always return your calls, but don't phone me again."

—New York Yankees owner George Steinbrenner, to reporter

"Everybody knows he was good at the beginning, but he just went too far."

—Marge Schott, Cincinnati Reds owner, assessing Adolf Hitler during ESPN interview

"The pride and presence of a professional football team is far more important than 30 libraries."

—Former Cleveland Browns owner Art Modell, before he took team to Baltimore

"David Cone is in a class by himself with three or four other players."

—George Steinbrenner, on his ace pitcher

"There's no question I'm unpopular, and I felt I needed to get away. So I got in my car and pulled up to a Motel 6. They turned the light off."

—Chicago White Sox owner Jerry Reinsdorf, at his charity roast

"I imagine that would have been a hotter item if his head was in it."

—Ex-grid coach Jerry Glanville, upon hearing that Art Modell's Cleveland Stadium toilet went for $2,700 during pre-stadium teardown auction

"If you own your own arena and you own the major tenant, it's the next best thing to having sex, if you're having sex. If you're not having sex, it's the best thing."

—Harry Ornest, ex-St. Louis Blues and Toronto Argonauts owner and current Hollywood Park vice chairman, on benefits of sports ownership

"There's nothing in the world I wouldn't do for Walter O'Malley. There's nothing in the world he wouldn't do for me. That's the way it is. We go through life doing nothing for each other."

—Gene Autry, California Angels owner, describing relationship with his Los Angeles Dodgers counterpart

"I'm not a win-at-all-costs guy. Winning isn't everything. It's second to breathing."

—George Steinbrenner

Chapter 15

DOLLARS & CENTS

"The minister should have said for richer and for richer."

—Seattle Sonics guard Gary Payton, reflecting back on his 1997 wedding and signing of his 7-year, $87.5 million contract

"It's like you're playing Monopoly and he's got all the little houses. You land on him and he just says, 'Give me all your damn money.'"

—Orlando Magic guard Anthony Bowie, explaining what it's like to guard Michael Jordan

"If I run out of money, Happy Meals go up to $2.99."

—Mike Pegram, owner of 1998 Kentucky Derby winner Real Quiet and 22 McDonald's franchises, on his financial participation in sport of kings

"We had a small wager, but the outcome did not affect the Forbes ranking."

—Berkshire Hathaway chairman Warren Buffett, on financial ramifications of round of golf with fellow billionaire Bill Gates of Microsoft

"Let me give you an idea how much money that is. . . by the time he gets a sign from his brain to scratch his groin, he's made $1,600."

—Jay Leno, analyzing value of Ken Griffey Jr.'s
$8.5-million-per-year contract

"I think I'm the highest paid baggage handler in the world."

—Indiana Pacers rookie Austin Croshere, on "earning" over $1 million while being mostly relegated to the bench and airports

"I'm just going to be an announcer, but I told them if they doubled my pay, they could throw me out of the ring—as long as they throw me headfirst, of course."

—Ex-baseball star Pete Rose, on involvement in "Wrestle Mania" featuring boxer Mike Tyson

"He's finally earning his money."

—Cincinnati pitcher Mark Portugal, after Reds' G.M. Jim Bowden temporarily joined stadium grounds crew and cleaned up around second base

"Ninety percent I'll spend on good times, women and Irish whiskey. The other 10 percent I'll probably waste."

—Tug McGraw, Philadelphia Phillies reliever, on plans for his salary

"It was like Bobby Brady just won the lottery."

—Billy Beane, Oakland A's assistant G.M., on shortstop and all-around nice guy Mike Bordick inking a $1 million, one-year contract

"I would—for the right amount of sushi."

—Pittsburgh Pirates outfielder Andy Van Slyke, asked if he would ever play in Japan

"I'm not really a free agent, but I'm very affordable."

—Placekicker Nick Lowery, 41, regarding his status after release by New York Jets

"Ostertag had asked for a $2 refund after renting 'Kazam.'"

—Comic Chris Rock, explaining his version of incident where Los Angeles Laker Shaquille O'Neal slapped Utah's Greg Ostertag

Chapter 16

LOCATION, LOCATION, LOCATION

"This is the greatest country in America."

—Bill Peterson, former Florida State and
Houston Oilers grid coach

**"We used to do charity exhibitions. After
one of these, I come out feeling so beat up,
I say, 'I don't even know, is that the sun or
moon up there?' Rocky [Graziano] says,
'I don't know. I'm not from around here.'"**

—Jake LaMotta, ex-middleweight champ and part-time comic

"Daniel Boone would have a tough time finding this place. The population is about 250. That's counting the pregnant people twice."

—Florida Marlins hurler David Weathers, describing hometown of Five Point, Tenn.

"I really love playing and living in New York. There's such a high energy here. Everybody's fighting for that same cab."

—Hockey star Wayne Gretzky, during his days with New York Rangers

"It's very difficult to drive a pickup truck from Lubbock to Hawaii."

—Iowa coach Hayden Fry, downplaying accounts that Alamo Bowl foe Texas Tech preferred Aloha Bowl berth

"That thing had to stop in Albuquerque to refuel."

—Colorado Rockies outfielder Larry Walker, on teammate Andres Galarraga's tape-measured 529-foot homer

". . . the largest ever to see a team sports event in the state of Las Vegas."

—ABC football announcer Mark Jones, a Toronto native, on WAC title contest crowd of 41,238

"Miami is so tough, they use Mace as a breath-freshener down there. . . . The cats only have six lives."

—Orlando Magic G.M. Pat Williams, anticipating playoff series against Miami Heat

"Philly fans are so mean that one Easter Sunday when the players staged an Easter-egg hunt for their kids, the fans booed the kids who didn't find any eggs."

—Bob Uecker

"Everyone in our league lives where they live because they can't sell their home or they've been relocated in the witness protection program."

—Rick Majerus, Utah Utes hoop coach,
on Western Athletic Conference

"First of all, it's way over on the other side of the field."

—David Justice, assessing his move from right to left field after
joining Cleveland from Atlanta

"I found a mound-mine map. You know, like a gold-mine map. It had a lot of little dots showing me how to get out to the mound."

—Roger McDowell, Los Angeles Dodgers reliever, finally called upon to pitch after 10 days on bench

"In Wrigley Field, I feel like King Kong. Here, I feel like Donkey Kong."

—St. Louis Cardinals infielder Gary Gaetti, on failing to hit ball out of Comiskey Park infield in game against White Sox

"It takes us three hours just to get Yinka [Dare] through customs. When they asked him what country he was arriving from, he said, 'USDA.'"

—New Jersey Nets forward Jayson Williams,
on entering Canada for NBA games

"It's like connecting the Atlantic with the Pacific."

—Philadelphia Flyer Eric Lindros, locating an appropriate
description of more-than-220-pound teammates 6-foot-6
Kjell Samuelson and 6-foot-3 Chris Therien

Chapter 17

MEASURING SHTICK

"He hit a pop-up against us one day that went so high, all nine guys on our team called for it."

—Florida Marlins coach Rich Donnelly, on Mark McGwire

"Put them all together and you'd have one person."

—Miami Heat center John Salley, summing up Cleveland Cavaliers coaching staff of Mike Fratello (5-foot-8), Ron Rothstein (5-foot-8) and Sidney Lowe (6-foot)

"Some are tall and some are small. Some are fat and some are thin."

—UC-Davis football coach Bob Briggs, describing dimensions of opponent Central Washington Wildcats before Aggies' 32–6 triumph

"Hello, everybody, and welcome to Two Rivers Stadium."

—San Francisco Giants broadcaster Hank Greenwald, after told to shorten his pre-game introduction at Three Rivers Stadium

"Some of it is over my head, and I'm 6-10."

—Marty Conlon, Milwaukee Bucks forward, on an NBA labor accord

"The bases are too high."

—John Canelosi, 5-foot-9 utility player for the Florida Marlins, on why he stumbled twice and fell over first base on ground balls

"That was like playing Wilt Chamberlain one-on-one."

—Seattle Mariners shortstop Alex Rodriguez, sizing up 6-foot-11 Ryan Anderson after facing his 99-mph delivery in spring training

"I was the Director of Vertical Transportation."

—Dave Snyder, Cincinnati teacher and ex-Riverfront Stadium elevator operator

"Up and down."

—Houston Rockets guard Vernon Maxwell, asked by coach Don Chaney for one-word summary of his performance during 1992 season

"The boss was pretty happy. He found someone who could wash roofs on vans."

—Zdeno Chara, 6-foot-9 New York Islanders defenseman,
on his summer car-wash job

"I saw him hit a ball in Knoxville that's still in orbit. We now have 10 planets."

—Cincinnati Red Steve Gibralter, on seeing teammate
Mike Kelly crush a ball during rehab assignment at
Class AA Chattanooga

Chapter 18

FOOD FOR THOUGHT

"Hey, I was only into finger sandwiches."

—Ex-Cardinals guard Conrad Dobler, who once bit opponent during grid game, downplaying any comparisons between him and Mike Tyson

"He can't cook."

—Michael Chang, asked after loss to Pete Sampras if his opponent had any weaknesses

"I had frog legs for my appetizer. That's why I'm so jumpy."

—Dallas Cowboys guard Nate Newton, during week of Super Bowl XXX

"It's really expensive. I don't know why. It tastes just like regular dirt."

—Golfer Jesper Parnevik, on eating volcanic dust
to cleanse his system

"My grandmother told me it was good for colds. It sure blows out those sinuses."

—Journeyman outfielder Kevin Mitchell,
on why he eats Vick's VapoRub

"I'm on a diet of bananas and seaweed. It doesn't make me a better player, but I'm a better swimmer."

—Gordon Strachan, Conventry soccer player–manager
in England's Premier League

"Major league baseball players finally resumed playing games. Do you know what I miss most about baseball? The pine tar, the resin, the grass, the dirt—and that's just in the hot dogs."

—David Letterman

"Oops."

—Boston Red Sox outfielder Jose Canseco, after tipping scales at 241 pounds on first day of 1997 spring training

"You look like you would have been a pretty good player at one time. About 100 biscuits ago."

—Referee Derek Stafford, to heckler at Sacramento Arco Arena

"I'm going to be in every weight-loss program available after football—I'll be into liposuction and ab-crunchers, and if that doesn't work, then I'm just going to stay in bed eating and have them bury me in a piano."

—Massive Dallas Cowboys offensive guard Nate Newton, on looking forward to life after his NFL career

"You mix two jiggers of Scotch to one jigger of Metrecal. So far I've lost five pounds and my driver's license."

—Former baseball manager Rocky Bridges, on his favorite diet drink

"Yeah, but me and the boys are eating ice-cream cones right now. I'll call you when we're done."

—Veteran NASCAR crew chief Henry Hyde, when driver Buddy Baker radioed to ask if he could pit due to handling problem

"The cream always rises to the top. I'm a good example of that . . . not exactly whipped cream. I'm kind of an ugly foam."

—Rex Hudler, California Angels utility player

"I love Chinese food."

—Heavyweight boxer Bruce Seldon, asked to say something to people of Japan during interview with Japanese TV station

"Nothing absorbs shocks like animal tissue."

—Team official Yvan Varmol, on why Tour de France
competitors stick steak in their pants for butt protection
during long race stages

**"He moves through a nine-hole course the
way a meal moves through a python."**

—Golfer David Owen, on his club's slowest duffer

**"I was mixing up my vitamin formula with
my hitting formula. I was taking one-a-days."**

—Paul Molitor, Toronto Blue Jays designated hitter,
on his season

Chapter 19

NOTHING LIKE EXPERIENCE

"I've got to wear more sun block."

—New York Giants quarterback Dave Brown, asked what he learned while sitting out preseason game on sidelines

"We've created a monster. Now he wants to study more than practice."

—Coach Dean Smith, on North Carolina player who returned after low grades kept him ineligible for a year

"I see three baseballs, but I only swing at the middle one."

—Paul Waner, Hall of Famer and former Pittsburgh Pirates outfielder, on using an educated guess to hit after drinking

"I'm a natural. I was the captain of the Safety Patrol in the second grade."

—Pro golfer Ben Crenshaw, U.S. Ryder Cup team captain, extolling his leadership experience

"Joe was always into books, anything to get an edge. Sometimes it was like a philosophy class. 'If a tree falls in New York, will Todd Zeile hit the curveball?' Stuff like that."

—Montreal catcher Darrin Fletcher, on former Expo pitching coach Joe Kerrigan

"Because that's my calculator."

—Sports information director Doug Tammaro, when Arizona State hoop coach Bill Frieder complained he couldn't figure out why hotel-room TV "remote control" wasn't working

"Dick brings a lot to the table with his experience. It has been a learning experience already. In training camp, we learned the right way to peel bananas."

—Denver Nuggets coach Bernie Bickerstaff, on adding veteran Dick Motta as assistant coach

"I'm in favor of it, as long as it's multiple choice."

—Los Angeles Laker Kurt Rambis, on his opinion of drug tests

"Seven years is a long time in one place. I almost spent that much time getting through college."

—Seven-year Los Angeles Kings assistant coach Cap Raeder, after getting fired along with coach Barry Melrose

"We might have to start piercing nipples by then."

—Punter Todd Sauerbrun, who got third earring in left ear to mark third year with Chicago Bears, on plans if he became 15-year NFL veteran

Chapter 20

HAIR YE, HAIR YE

"It's an aura from God."

—Boxing promoter Don King, on his famous stand-up hair

"They couldn't get through the concrete. I think Tim [Hardaway] broke his hand trying."

—Miami coach Pat Riley, after Heat players attempted to mess up his slicked down hair following his 800th NBA triumph

"It looks like an inkblot test I get at my psychiatrist."

—Chicago Bulls center Bill Wennington, describing Dennis Rodman's latest creative hair-color patterns

"I really do believe he's having an All-Star season, although he wasn't selected, and I prefer him as a platinum blond."

—NBA Commissioner David Stern, on Dennis Rodman

"When I figured out it was actually older than Tiger Woods."

—Brad Bryant, 43-year-old PGA Tour competitor, explaining reason he shaved off his mustache

"He's probably one of the best pressure players of all time. And there would finally be someone on the team balder than me."

—Dave Babych, Vancouver defenseman, on positive feelings after hearing that Canucks were about to sign free-agent center Mark Messier

"His hair was blowing in the breeze—and he was too proud to chase it."

—Clemson basketball coach Cliff Ellis, telling charity roast audience about first time he saw Dick Vitale

"If my hair can look better than his, I'll have it made."

—Mike Ditka, then with NBC, on Jimmy Johnson joining Fox

"You know that in golf, you've got to aerate the greens once in a while. Well, I'm just aerating my head. Maybe with the air getting at it, I'll get smarter."

—Anaheim Mighty Ducks coach Ron Wilson, trying to explain his much shorter haircut

"Short, slow, hairy."

—Northwestern wide receiver Brian Musso, asked to describe
himself in three words

**"They had a buy-one-get-one-free deal.
I took both of them at the same time."**

—Vancouver Canuck Alexander Mogilny, on his short
and bad-looking haircut

Chapter 21

CLOTHES LINES

"I was kind of hoping to make the swimsuit issue."

—Pat Summitt, Tennessee women's basketball coach,
upon making cover of "Sports Illustrated"

"Hey, Appier, pitch faster! By the time you get done, my clothes will be out of style!"

—Pro golfer Chi Chi Rodriguez, to Kansas City Royals pitcher
Kevin Appier during game with Cleveland

"I can't believe how physical the NBA is getting lately. Shaquille O'Neal—what is he, 320 pounds—comes down the court and crashes into Dennis Rodman. Luckily, Dennis was wearing a padded bra, so he's okay."

—Jay Leno

"If it would have been the backstroke, I obviously would have stopped."

—Swimmer Matt Zelen, St. John's (Minn.) University, stripped of his victory because his swimsuit came off during race

"I spent the whole day worrying about whether someone would see my underwear."

—Golfer Nancy Lopez, explaining how broken zipper on first hole might have cost her 1977 U.S. Open title over Hollis Stacy

"Attention, please: Will the people behind the rail in left field please remove their clothing."

—Brooklyn Dodgers public address announcer Tex Rickard, asking fans at Ebbets Field not to drape jackets over railing

"I understand he wants to play naked? In his last game? It probably would be."

—NBA Commissioner David Stern, on Dennis Rodman's talk of stripping off his uniform as he leaves court in final game

"I'd leave my helmet on but take the whole uniform off. I'll strip down to my jock and run to the sidelines."

—Emmitt Smith, Dallas Cowboys running back, on plans to skirt new NFL edict penalizing players who remove their helmet to celebrate

"I think he did it in honor of the University of Wisconsin. Either that or Dr. Seuss."

—Tampa Bay coach Tony Dungy, on funky red-and-white striped knee socks worn by safety Charles Mincy to practice

"We're just everyday professional people who want to get out, put on a red dress and run."

—Don Kresal, member of DC Hash House Harriers, which put on its 4th annual Red Dress Run

"We're so young, we've decided to dress only seven players on the road. We're pretty confident the other five can dress themselves."

—Charlie Just, women's hoop coach at Louisville's Bellarmine College, on squad's inexperience

"If clothes make the man, why are lifeguards so popular?"

—Volney Meece, editor of "Football Writers Monthly"

"The winds were blowing 50 mph and gusting to 70. I hit a 3-par with my hat."

—Pro golfer Chi Chi Rodriguez

"If I had on the right shoes, I would've caught it."

—Outfielder Michael Jordan, on a home-run ball hit barely over his head

"I look like pause on the VCR."

—Chicago Bulls guard Steve Kerr, on his black sneakers making him look slow

"They're nice. We've got Rudolph on the front."

—Milwaukee guard Lee Mayberry, assessing new Bucks' jersey featuring large deer head

"I think Clem has underwear older than Steve Lavin."

—Basketball analyst Al McGuire, sizing up age difference between Minnesota coach Clem Haskins and UCLA coach Lavin in NCAA tourney game

"At least now I can say I had a jersey retired."

—Newly signed Dallas center Oliver Miller, after weighing in at 342 pounds and splitting open jersey in his Mavericks debut

Chapter 22

PHYSICAL ATTRIBUTES

"This isn't a body. It's a cruel family joke."

—Philadelphia Phillies strikeout artist Curt Schilling, on his
6-foot-4, 234-pound physique

"I'd just like to put it behind me."

—Tennessee quarterback Peyton Manning, questioned about
training-room incident in which he allegedly "mooned"
teammate in view of female trainer

**"We had to fill in the ovaries recently,
because people kept getting stuck in them."**

—French golf club director Florian Teves, regarding La Salle,
first course design based on female anatomy

"Hell, I'm more attractive than Buffy."

—Harry Caray, learning that WGN was reducing
1998 Cubs broadcasts by 52 games to air shows such as
"Buffy the Vampire Slayer"

"One was a clown. The other was a hippie. Me? I didn't dress up. My face is scary enough."

—Esa Tikkanen, Vancouver Canucks left winger, about taking
his daughters around for trick-or-treat on Halloween

"My ultimate dream is to get a pot belly. I just want to sit around and relax and not focus on what I have to do the next day."

—Michael Jordan, to TV interviewer Keenen Ivory Wayans

"You don't want to walk back to the dugout with your head between your legs."

—Dmitri Young, St. Louis Cardinals rookie first sacker

"The photographer doesn't say 'Give us your best side.' He says, 'Give us your least-damaged side.'"

—Brendan Shanahan, St. Louis Blues left winger, after posing for "GQ" photo

"On a windy day, I don't know which side of my face my nose is going to be on."

—Austin Ice Bats defenseman Kyle Haviland, whose nose had been broken eight times in hockey fights

"You know you're on the Senior Tour when your back goes out more than you do."

—Golfer Bob Brue

"Inside, I'm skinny and quick."

—Green Bay Packers nose tackle Gilbert Brown, weighing in between 325 and 360 pounds, on prep sprinter days

"I used to be a Chippendale. Now I'm a Clydesdale."

—Houston Rockets forward Charles Barkley, on impact of growing older

"That's fine with me. . . . I'm a pig. I can roll in the mud with the best of them."

—Robert "Pig" Goff, New Orleans Saints nose tackle, accepting challenge of being blocked by two linemen

"No way. I felt like van Gogh without his ear."

—Detroit Piston Grant Long, on whether he'd play another game without his goggles after losing them

"He didn't have his teeth in."

—Chicago Blackhawks defenseman Eric Weinrich, grateful for one thing after New Jersey Devil Doug Gilmour bit him on hand

"I got tired of pulling out my wallet and showing everyone photos."

—Then-Baltimore Orioles pitcher David Wells, explaining decision to get tattoo of son, Brandon, on his arm

"Why would I have a tattoo of someone else?"

—Clifford Robinson, Portland Trail Blazers forward, on having tattoo of himself on right biceps

"My arm would have to go with the ball."

—Curt Schilling, Philadelphia Phillies pitcher, on whether he'd ever be able to throw a 100-mph fastball

"His feet and arms aren't working together."

—Seattle manager Lou Piniella, on reason for benching
error-prone third baseman Russ Davis, who made 10 errors
in 30 games

"When it comes to that stomach, you don't expect to stop it. You can only hope to contain it."

—Dan Bernstein, WSCR Radio in Chicago, discussing waistline
of Seattle Sonics coach George Karl

"That's the size of my left calf."

—Sumo wrestler Akebono, on his 6-foot-8, 516-pound
body versus 4-foot-10, 82-pounder Tara Lipinski,
Olympic figure-skating gold medalist

"My knee's only a few months old, my back is only 17, and I recently got a new hip. I might be too young now."

—Golfer George Archer, on his number of replaced body parts possibly impacting his Senior Tour status

"Pat lacked tactile dexterity."

—Minnesota catcher Matt Walbeck, on reason Twins pitcher Pat Mahomes was off his game

"His upper body is built like Mr. Olympia. And his lower body is built like Kathie Lee Gifford."

—Charles Barkley, on Houston Rockets teammate Kevin Willis

"We're physically not physical enough."

—Louisville basketball coach Denny Crum,
after 22-point loss to St. John's

"I was going to find Evander Holyfield's ear."

—Chuck Knoblauch, Minnesota Twins second baseman, on why
he thought about heading to Las Vegas during All-Star break

Chapter 23

AILMENTS &
TREATMENTS

"Mike Marshall went back to L.A. to get cocaine in his foot."

—Harry Caray, who meant Novocain

"For us, ultrasound [treatment] was putting your foot on the radio and turning it to an FM station."

—Johnny Kerr, Chicago Bulls broadcast analyst, comparing therapy available during his playing days to that of today

"We're just fortunate it wasn't diaper rash."

—Ted Green, Edmonton coach, after his young Oilers squad lost Jason Arnott for a game from tonsillitis

"It's a pain in the butt."

—Kevin Duckworth, Los Angeles Clippers center,
describing his foot injury

"I just hope I never get kicked in the groin."

—John Elway, after his torn biceps tendon was illustrated
in local newspapers

"My groin has no comment."

—Al Leiter, Florida Marlins pitcher, discouraging any
pictures of his injury

"He was diagnosed with tuberculosis, which is unusual after hitting his head on the water cooler."

—Broadcaster Ralph Kiner, trying to make heads or tails out of medical status of New York Mets pitcher Jason Isringhausen

"Now I know what it feels like to be an airhead."

—Charles Barkley, emerging from hyperbaric chamber, which pumps more oxygen into brain and body to speed healing

"They checked my head out and found I have a brain. That was real encouraging."

—Scott Mitchell, Detroit Lions quarterback, on tests run after he suffered from dizziness during game

"Sometimes, even if you spend lots of money on a baseball team, it won't win. Things happen, injuries. Guys fall down. One of your pitchers can get one of those rotary cuffs."

—Ted Turner

"He lubed it, oiled it, filtered it. I opted for the new-car scent instead of apple cinnamon."

—Roger McDowell, Baltimore Orioles reliever, explaining maintenance job an orthopedic surgeon did on his shoulder

"They've had so many injuries, they get to park their team bus in the handicapped zone."

—Basketball commentator George Raveling, describing Washington State's injury-plagued squad

"When I left, I said I'd like to give Harold something to commemorate our five years together. But I never could figure out how to get an ulcer framed."

—Orlando Magic G.M. Pat Williams, on leaving the employ of then-Philadelphia 76ers owner Harold Katz

"Maybe I'm not getting enough saltwater to my brain."

—Frankie Hejduk, U.S. men's soccer team member and California surfer, on his hamstring injuries

"My people aren't allowed to have hamstrings."

—San Francisco Giants broadcaster Hank Greenwald, who is Jewish, commenting on player's pulled hamstring

"It just goes to show what happens to those guys who wear high heels."

—Broadcaster Marv Albert, on Dennis Rodman's knee injury

"He's not going to get sick. Germs are scared of him."

—Ex–New York Yankee Reggie Jackson, explaining why slugger Albert Belle had never been on disabled list

"As long as they don't put a cast on my tongue, I'm OK."

—Broadcaster Dick Vitale, downplaying concern regarding his broken wrist

"I've never seen anyone on the disabled list with pulled fat."

—Stout Chicago Cubs closer Rod Beck, explaining why his weight was non-issue

"They can't make a dislocated shoe."

—Charles Oakley, New York Knicks forward, on why it's hard to play with dislocated toe

Chapter 24

IT'S LIKE THIS...

"Well, we got ahead and then we got behind and we got ahead and then we got behind and then we got ahead and then we got behind and we got ahead again."

—Wyoming football coach Joe Tiller, on wild 45–42 victory over Northern Iowa

"It's a trifle warm, but it's not as hot as my putter or my first wristwatch."

—Pro golfer Chi Chi Rodriguez

"You win some, lose some and wreck some."

—NASCAR driver Dale Earnhardt, summing up his racing philosophy

"It's like being a ballet dancer—tight pants, a little contact and a whole lot of kicking."

—BYU placekicker Jason Chaffetz, on his position

"I've always said a home run is just a baseball that goes over the fence."

—Slugger Mark McGwire, who regularly pounds 'em more than "just over" the fence

"It was like the Pope not being allowed to say Mass."

—Buffalo Bills linebacker Chris Spielman, on not being able to work out for more than two months due to neck injury

"Deceiving runner. He's slower than he looks."

—Former TV broadcaster and major-league catcher Joe Garagiola, recalling scouting report he read on himself

"I look up in the stands and I see them miss balls, too."

—Devon White, Florida Marlins center-fielder, after fans booed him for dropping fly ball

"Actually, I'm not a complainer— I'm a whiner."

—Danny Ainge, asked during his NBA playing career about his reputation

"I'm a four-wheel-drive-pickup type of guy, and so is my wife."

—Mike Greenwell, Boston Red Sox outfielder, summing up his personality

"Right now I'd bet he feels like the luckiest boy on the face of the earth."

—MSNBC's Michael Ventre, after Gehrig Schilling's dad, Phillies hurler Curt Schilling, got contract extension worth over $15 million

"Looks like Cone burned the Candaele at both ends."

—Broadcaster Tim McCarver, after New York Yankee pitcher David Cone fanned Houston's Casey Candaele on three pitches

Chapter 25

THAT'S
ENTERTAINMENT

"He hit that so hard, he knocked the frogs off the Budweiser sign."

—Indians center-fielder Brian Giles, amazed by Mark McGwire's home-run blast at Jacobs Field

"I told the producer I'd like to play myself. He said, 'Nah, you're not the type.'"

—Retired boxing champion Jake LaMotta, about "Raging Bull," film based on his life

"He asked me one day, 'What do you guys do at halftime?' That's when I knew it was going to be one long damn movie."

—Ex-Philadelphia Phillies infielder John Kruk, who had player role in "The Fan," on talking baseball with director Tony Scott

"Acting with Michael Jordan is like bowling with Picasso."

—"Seinfeld" actor Wayne "Newman" Knight, summing up his "Space Jam" movie experience with Jordan

"Let's just say that if Disneyland is ever looking for someone to wear the Goofy costume, I've got the perfect candidate."

—Larry Andersen, Philadelphia minor-league coach and former major-league hurler, describing Phillies rookie starter Mike Grace

"How come this town doesn't have the Cartoon Network? I looked all over the dial for it."

—Minnesota Timberwolves forward Kevin Garnett,
to Vancouver, B.C., media

"We can't even get on Nickelodeon."

—Cleveland Cavalier Tyrone Hill, lamenting team's lack of
national television exposure during 1996 season

"The bottom line is entertaining the fans, and watching some of our pitchers hit is pretty funny."

—Minnesota Twins skipper Tom Kelly, describing results
of interleague play

"I don't care if you don't like the Packers and you hate cheese. Everybody could use cheesehead toilet paper."

—Spokesman Chris Becker of Foamation Inc., which makes cheeseheads, toilet seats and cheese-related items

"That makes sense, to put a hockey player on a can of soup. It's probably the only thing they can eat, without teeth."

—Jay Leno, after Wayne Gretzky became first person to go on Campbell's soup label

"I'm calling on Max Factor and Revlon. She can promote a rouge that don't bruise."

—Don King, seeking sponsor for female boxer Christy Martin

"My mother and Captain Kangaroo."

—Notre Dame offensive tackle Aaron Taylor, naming people
that most influenced his life

"No, thank you. I'm trying to quit."

—Green Bay Packers quarterback Brett Favre,
turning down makeup powder before on-camera
interview with ABC's Al Michaels

**"Think of the promotional possibilities.
On Reynolds-Rapp night, the first 25,000
fans get free tinfoil."**

—Florida Marlin Jeff Conine, on potential for matchup between
hurlers Shane Reynolds of Houston and Pat Rapp of Florida

"It's been a very good year. Excuse me, it's been a very fine year."

—Indy car driver Scott Pruett, who had Firestone as a sponsor

"The proposed ban on outdoor cigarette advertising will have an effect on [NASCAR] Winston Cup racing. Next year, it will be known as Nicoderm Patch Cup racing."

—Bret Lewis of KFWB radio in Southern California

"Let's check the scoreboard, brought to you by Subway sandwiches. It's still there."

—San Francisco broadcaster Hank Greenwald, during day when no other games were in progress

Chapter 26

DANCIN' TO THE MUSIC

**"They didn't call you for taunting.
They called you for bad dancing."**

—Tampa Bay defensive end Brad Culpepper, after Chidi
Ahanotu was penalized for taunting during sack dance over
Atlanta quarterback Chris Chandler

**"He's a terrific guy and the world's
quietest person. The night he broke
[Lou] Gehrig's record, he went out and
painted the town beige."**

—Billy Ripken, on his brother, Cal

**"We should lead the league in good
national anthem singers."**

—Nashville Predators G.M. Dave Poile, on benefits of
expansion team's location in country-music capital

"I'm training just to get through the anthem."

—Phoenix Sun Joe Kleine, who fainted during "The Star Spangled Banner" before a game, on his playoff goals

"We have black players, white players, a Mormon and four Yugoslavians. Our toughest decision isn't what offense or defense to run, but what type of warm-up music to play."

—Wagner College hoop coach Tim Capstraw, on team's cultural diversity

"I knew it was going to be a long season when, on opening day during the national anthem, one of my players turns to me and says, 'Every time I hear that song, I have a bad game.'"

—Manager Jim Leyland, recalling one of his challenging seasons at Pittsburgh Pirates helm

Chapter 27

HOBBY TIME

"I couldn't get my golf clubs in the Ferrari."

—World Series MVP Livan Hernandez of Florida Marlins,
on why he traded his Ferrari for a Mercedes

"It took me 17 years to get 3,000 hits. I did it in one afternoon on the golf course."

—Hank Aaron

"I'm not crazy about running. I just do it to keep in shape for fishing."

—Donald Gowdy, 66, after victory in 5,000 meters in his
age-group at North Carolina State Games

"It looks cool. You know, the chicks and everything. The one here, I got to play with the siren."

—Mike Holmgren, Green Bay Packers coach,
on his motivation for riding motorcycles

"It was a laser like you'd have on a hunting rifle. I wasn't worried, though. I didn't think it was deer season."

—Boston Red Sox hurler Jim Corsi, after fan aimed laser beam
into his eyes at Yankee Stadium

"As an ice facility chain, we're only as strong as our weakest rink."

—New York Ranger Luc Robitaille, partner in firm operating
an ice-rink chain

"I may have to take up golf. I saw Jason [Kidd] play. He hit the ball right in the water. I know I can do that."

—Phoenix Suns guard Kevin Johnson, mulling his retirement activities

"I think there's something very tranquil about whizzing a golf ball past a heifer's head on Sunday afternoon."

—Anson Tebbetts, on benefits of playing golf on his dairy-farm course in Cabot, Vermont

"I play like I pitch. I hit sinkers, sliders and curveballs."

—Ariel Prieto, Oakland A's pitcher, summing up his slowly developing golf game

"They have 57 golf courses down here [in Palm Springs area], and he doesn't know which one he's going to play until after his first tee shot."

—Bob Hope, on former President Gerald Ford's golf adventures

Chapter 28

TAKE MY ADVICE

"Why buy good luggage? You only use it when you travel."

—Yogi Berra

"When you tell your mother, make sure she's unarmed."

—Lou Holtz's counsel after son, Skip, told him he wanted to be a football coach

"He's kind of filled me in on how to moon helicopters."

—Brett Favre, during his first Super Bowl experience, on advice of teammate and ex-Chicago Bear Jim McMahon

"My house is only 21 miles from the park. I've already told my wife, 'When he comes to bat, keep the dogs in and stay out of the pool.'"

—Rich Donnelly, Florida Marlins coach, on Mark McGwire hitting at Arizona Diamondbacks stadium in Phoenix

"It runs the gamut of close your left eye, close your right eye, close both eyes, turn sideways and putt backward."

—Tom Watson, on interesting advice received during putting slump

"Tie an anvil to his ankle."

—Bill Wennington, Chicago Bulls backup center, on how to stop Shaquille O'Neal

"Don't hit it to me."

—Slugger Jose Canseco, suggesting way for team
to improve its defense

**"During the years ahead, when you come
to a fork in the road, take it."**

—Yogi Berra, offering guidance at college graduation ceremony

**"The best way to avoid ballplayers is
to go to a good restaurant."**

—Broadcaster Tim McCarver

"If a guy is a good fastball hitter, does that mean I should throw him a bad fastball?"

—Veteran hurler Larry Andersen

"Always go to other people's funerals. Otherwise, they won't go to yours."

—Yogi Berra

Chapter 29

HODGEPODGE

"I wasn't mad. I just tossed it into the water because I didn't ever want to see it again."

—John Daly, after pitching his driver into water hazard
at Scandinavian Masters

"I don't know what's wrong. Lately, I've had to psych myself up just to go out there and punch somebody in the face. That's not me."

—Matthew Barnaby, Buffalo Sabres enforcer, after benched by
coach Lindy Ruff during game with Edmonton

"Gee, I don't know. Are my grounders going harder than usual?"

—Kent Herbek, Minnesota Twins first sacker,
on whether ball was livelier

"He hits the ball so hard, the guy on deck can score."

—Mike Stanley, on Boston Red Sox teammate Mo Vaughn

"It's so slow you could swing twice."

—Red Sox catcher Scott Hatteberg,
on Pedro Martinez's change-up

"I went to church the other day to pray for our pitchers. But there weren't enough candles."

—Cincinnati Reds manager Jack McKeon, on his pitching staff

"The UPS guy made a very nice presentation."

—Toronto Blue Jays catcher Charlie O'Brien, after finally getting World Series ring won previous season with Atlanta Braves

"It'll be an honor to squat in his footsteps."

—Catcher Josh Paul, number two draft pick of Chicago White Sox and big fan of Carlton Fisk, team's former backstop

"You don't have to pedal uphill."

—Three-time Tour de France champion Greg LeMond, now pursuing an auto-racing career, on difference between the two sports

"The thing you cannot forget is that there isn't anything wrong with winning ugly. As a matter of fact, there isn't anything wrong with being ugly—as long as you're successful."

—Lou Holtz